USC Son Petitioning Parent

Sample Petition for a Grown USC Child Petitioning His or Her Parent for Lawful Permanent Residency

Attorney Brian D. Lerner

LAW OFFICES OF BRIAN D. LERNER A PROFESSIONAL CORPORATION

ATTORNEY DRAFTED IMMIGRATION PETITIONS

By

Brian D. Lerner

Attorney at Law

Disclaimer and Terms of Use:

Effort has been made to ensure that the information in this book is accurate and complete. However, the author and the publisher do not warrant that this particular petition will mirror or be exactly as your situation. There has not been any attorney-client agreement created by the purchase of this petition or application. No legal advice has occurred. The cases, regulations and/or statutes cited may change at any time without notice.

ISBN: 978-1-958990-19-3

INTRODUCTION

There are a multitude of different immigration petitions and applications. They are complex and full of requirements. Obviously, it would be best to hire an immigration attorney to best prepare the petitions and applications. However, this can certainly cost thousands of dollars.

The next best option is to get a sample of the petition written by an experienced immigration attorney. The samples cost a fraction what would be charged by an immigration attorney. However, while the reader has to alter, amend and change the parts of the sample petition to reflect their actual situation, it is a fantastic roadmap for them to use. If the reader has purchased the entire petition or application, they will have real live samples of cover letters, forms, declarations, affidavits and the necessary exhibits to use. The samples come from real cases and the names of those clients have been redacted to protect the privacy of that person or corporation.

These are petitions and applications that have been drafted by an experienced immigration attorney with over 25 years of experience. Get the benefits of that experience without the costs.

CONTENTS

About the Law Offices of Brian D. Lerner

The Law Offices of Brian D. Lerne, APC. The law practice consists of Immigration and Nationality Law and everything involved with and regarding immigration which includes citizenship, investment visas, family and employment visas, removal and deportation hearings, appeals, waivers, adjustment, consulate processing and all types of immigration and citizenship matters. Thousands of families have been reunited and/or permitted to stay in the U.S. and/or return to the U.S. because of the successful work of Immigration Attorney Brian D. Lerner.

This law offices handles all types of immigration cases including family based and employment based. Immigration issues range from immigration court proceedings to trying to fix what paralegals may have done that was neither correct nor proper. Foreign nationals must have experience lawyers admitted to practice law.

The Law Offices of Brian D. Lerner, APC, handles cases arising from business visas, work permits, Green Cards, non-immigrant visas, deportation, citizenship, appeals and all areas of immigration. The Law Offices of Brian D. Lerner, APC does EB-5 Investor Visas, H-1B Specialty Occupation, L-1 Intracompany Transferee, E-2 Treaty Investor, E-1 Treaty Trader, O-1 Extraordinary Ability among others. Regarding immigrant visas for the Green Card, the firm does PERM and advanced degree PERM, Family Petitions, and Extraordinary Alien Petitions. In addition to affirmative petitions, the Law Firm represents people in people in deportation and removal hearings, including political asylum, withholding of removal, and convention against torture cases.

Brian D. Lerner has been certified as an expert in Immigration & Nationality Law by the California State Bar, Board of Legal Specialization since 2000 and has been re-certified three times. He now passes on his decades of experience by allowing the Reader, Law Schools, Professors and other Immigration Attorneys to purchase sample petitions on every facet of Immigration Law.

About USC Son Petitioning Parent

Ready to Petition your Parent? In this case, are you a United States Citizen over 21 years old petitioning your mother or father. It will be considered an Immediate Relative Petition where there will be no visa waiting. You can move on to the next step the moment it is approved to either adjusting status or consulate processing. The first part must be done and must be done properly in order to ever proceed to the next part. Without a proper I-130 application there will never be a Green Card. If approved, then you could move onto the next step in the Immigration process. If not approved, it will take years of red tape. Remember, it is your responsibility to submit everything correctly. This sample I-130 Petition has everything necessary to give you the best chance possible to get an approval. Just input your own information and use the application as a guide. It has been prepared by an expert Immigration Attorney. Thus, this book will allow you to see a guide of how it is done, prepared and submitted.

ATTORNEY COVER LETTER

Law Offices of Brian D. Lerner

A PROFESSIONAL CORPORATION

CERTIFIED SPECIALIST IN IMMIGRATION AND NATIONALITY LAW
ADMITTED TO THE U.S. SUPREME COURT

LONG BEACH, CALIFORNIA
(562) 495-0554

CARSON, CALIFORNIA
(310) 684-5420

November 2, 2018

U.S. Citizenship and Immigration Services
ATTN: I-130
PO Box 21700
Phoenix, AZ 85036

RE: I-130, Petition for Alien Relative
Petitioner: [redacted]
Beneficiary: [redacted]

Dear Sir/Madam:

We hereby submit an I-130, Petition of Alien Relative, for [redacted] (hereinafter "Petitioner") on behalf of his mother [redacted] (hereinafter "Beneficiary").

Enclosed herein please find the following documents:

FORMS

Form:	**Description:**
G-28	Notice of Entry of Appearance as Attorney or Accredited Representative (Petitioner); and
I-130	Petition for Alien Relative with $535.00 Filing Fee.

EXHIBITS

Exhibits:	**Description:**
1.	Petitioner's Birth Certificate;
2.	Petitioner's Certificate of Naturalization;
3.	Beneficiary's Birth Certificate;
4.	Beneficiary's Foreign Passport; and
5.	Beneficiary's Visa and I-94.

Under the Immigration and Nationality Act ("INA") § 201 (b) (2) (A) (i), the Immediate Relatives, including children, spouses and parents, of a U.S. citizen may be petitioned for an immigrant visa, without being subjected to direct numerical limitations.

In the present case, Petitioner is a U.S. Citizen. Beneficiary is the mother of Petitioner. Therefore, Petitioner is qualified to file an Alien Relative Petition on behalf of his mother.

Based on the foregoing, we respectfully submit that the attached evidence shows the necessary relationship exists and that the instant I-130 should be approved.

Thank you for your consideration in this matter. Should you have any further questions, please feel free to contact our office at

FORMS

Notice of Entry of Appearance as Attorney or Accredited Representative

Department of Homeland Security

DHS Form G-28
OMB No. 1615-0105
Expires 05/31/2021

Part 1. Information About Attorney or Accredited Representative

1. USCIS Online Account Number (if any) ▶

Name of Attorney or Accredited Representative

2.a. Family Name (Last Name) [redacted]

2.b. Given Name (First Name) [redacted]

2.c. Middle Name [redacted]

Address of Attorney or Accredited Representative

3.a. Street Number and Name: 3233 E. Broadway

3.b. ☐ Apt. ☐ Ste. ☐ Flr.

3.c. City or Town: Long Beach

3.d. State: CA 3.e. ZIP Code: 90803

3.f. Province

3.g. Postal Code

3.h. Country

Contact Information of Attorney or Accredited Representative

4. Daytime Telephone Number: (562) 495-0554

5. Mobile Telephone Number (if any)

6. Email Address (if any) [redacted]

7. Fax Number (if any): (562) 608-8672

Part 2. Eligibility Information for Attorney or Accredited Representative

Select **all applicable** items.

1.a. ☒ I am an attorney eligible to practice law in, and a member in good standing of, the bar of the highest courts of the following states, possessions, territories, commonwealths, or the District of Columbia. If you need extra space to complete this section, use the space provided in **Part 6. Additional Information.**

Licensing Authority: Calif omia Supreme Court

1.b. Bar Number (if applicable) [redacted]

1.c. I (select only one box) ☒ am not ☐ am subject to any order suspending, enjoining, restraining, disbarring, or otherwise restricting me in the practice of law. If you are subject to any orders, use the space provided in **Part 6. Additional Information** to provide an explanation.

1.d. Name of Law Firm or Organization (if applicable): Law Offices of Brian D. Lerner, APC

2.a. ☐ I am an accredited representative of the following qualified nonprofit religious, charitable, social service, or similar organization established in the United States and recognized by the Department of Justice in accordance with 8 CFR part 1292.

2.b. Name of Recognized Organization

2.c. Date of Accreditation (mm/dd/yyyy)

3. ☐ I am associated with ______, the attorney or accredited representative of record who previously filed Form G-28 in this case, and my appearance as an attorney or accredited representative for a limited purpose is at his or her request.

4.a. ☐ I am a law student or law graduate working under the direct supervision of the attorney or accredited representative of record on this form in accordance with the requirements in 8 CFR 292.1(a)(2).

4.b. Name of Law Student or Law Graduate

Part 3. Notice of Appearance as Attorney or Accredited Representative

If you need extra space to complete this section, use the space provided in **Part 6. Additional Information**.

This appearance relates to immigration matters before (select **only one** box):

1.a. [X] U.S. Citizenship and Immigration Services (USCIS)

1.b. List the form numbers or specific matter in which appearance is entered.

I-130

2.a. [ ] U.S. Immigration and Customs Enforcement (ICE)

2.b. List the specific matter in which appearance is entered.

3.a. [ ] U.S. Customs and Border Protection (CBP)

3.b. List the specific matter in which appearance is entered.

4. Receipt Number (if any)

►

5. I enter my appearance as an attorney or accredited representative at the request of the (select **only one** box):

[ ] Applicant [X] Petitioner [ ] Requestor
[ ] Beneficiary/Derivative [ ] Respondent (ICE, CBP)

Information About Client (Applicant, Petitioner, Requestor, Beneficiary or Derivative, Respondent, or Authorized Signatory for an Entity)

6.a. Family Name (Last Name)

6.b. Given Name (First Name)

6.c. Middle Name

7.a. Name of Entity

7.b. Title of Authorized Signatory for Entity (if applicable)

8. Client's USCIS Online Account Number (if any)

►

9. Client's Alien Registration Number (A-Number) (if any)

► A-

Client's Contact Information

10. Daytime Telephone Number

11. Mobile Telephone Number (if any)

12. Email Address (if any)

Mailing Address of Client

NOTE: Provide the client's mailing address. **Do not** provide the business mailing address of the attorney or accredited representative **unless** it serves as the safe mailing address on the application or petition being filed with this Form G-28.

13.a. Street Number and Name

13.b. [ ] Apt. [ ] Ste. [ ] Flr.

13.c. City or Town Long Beach

13.d. State CA 13.e. ZIP Code 90806

13.f. Province

13.g. Postal Code

13.h. Country

USA

Part 4. Client's Consent to Representation and Signature

Consent to Representation and Release of Information

I have requested the representation of and consented to being represented by the attorney or accredited representative named in **Part 1.** of this form. According to the Privacy Act of 1974 and U.S. Department of Homeland Security (DHS) policy, I also consent to the disclosure to the named attorney or accredited representative of any records pertaining to me that appear in any system of records of USCIS, ICE, or CBP.

Part 4. Client's Consent to Representation and Signature (continued)

Options Regarding Receipt of USCIS Notices and Documents

USCIS will send notices to both a represented party (the client) and his, her, or its attorney or accredited representative either through mail or electronic delivery. USCIS will send all secure identity documents and Travel Documents to the client's U.S. mailing address.

If you want to have notices and/or secure identity documents sent to your attorney or accredited representative of record rather than to you, please select all applicable items below. You may change these elections through written notice to USCIS.

1.a. ☒ I request that USCIS send original notices on an application or petition to the U.S. business address of my attorney or accredited representative as listed in this form.

1.b. ☐ I request that USCIS send any secure identity document (Permanent Resident Card, Employment Authorization Document, or Travel Document) that I receive to the U.S. business address of my attorney or accredited representative (or to a designated military or diplomatic address in a foreign country (if permitted)).

NOTE: If your notice contains Form I-94, Arrival-Departure Record, USCIS will send the notice to the U.S. business address of your attorney or accredited representative. If you would rather have your Form I-94 sent directly to you, select **Item Number 1.c.**

1.c. ☐ I request that USCIS send my notice containing Form I-94 to me at my U.S. mailing address.

Signature of Client or Authorized Signatory for an Entity

2.a. Signature of Client or Authorized Signatory for an Entity

➡ [redacted]

2.b. Date of Signature (mm/dd/yyyy) 11/1/18

Part 5. Signature of Attorney or Accredited Representative

I have read and understand the regulations and conditions contained in 8 CFR 103.2 and 292 governing appearances and representation before DHS. I declare under penalty of perjury under the laws of the United States that the information I have provided on this form is true and correct.

1.a. [redacted]

1.b. Date of Signature (mm/dd/yyyy) 11/2/18

2.a. Signature of Law Student or Law Graduate

2.b. Date of Signature (mm/dd/yyyy)

Part 6. Additional Information

If you need extra space to provide any additional information within this form, use the space below. If you need more space than what is provided, you may make copies of this page to complete and file with this form or attach a separate sheet of paper. Type or print your name at the top of each sheet; indicate the **Page Number**, **Part Number**, and **Item Number** to which your answer refers; and sign and date each sheet.

1.a Family Name (Last Name) [redacted]

1.b. Given Name (First Name) [redacted]

1.c. Middle Name [redacted]

2.a. Page Number 2.b. Part Number 2.c. Item Number

2.d.

3.a. Page Number 3.b. Part Number 3.c. Item Number

3.d.

4.a. Page Number 4.b. Part Number 4.c. Item Number

4.d.

5.a. Page Number 5.b. Part Number 5.c. Item Number

5.d.

6.a. Page Number 6.b. Part Number 6.c. Item Number

6.d.

Petition for Alien Relative

Department of Homeland Security
U.S. Citizenship and Immigration Services

USCIS Form I-130
OMB No. 1615-0012
Expires 07/31/2018

For USCIS Use Only	Fee Stamp	Action Stamp
A-Number A-		
Initial Receipt		
Resubmitted		
Relocated	Section of Law/Visa Category	
Received	☐ 201(b) Spouse - IR-1/CR-1 ☐ 203(a)(1) Unm. S/D - F1-1 ☐ 203(a)(2)(B) Unm. S/D - F2-4	
Sent	☐ 201(b) Child - IR-2/CR-2 ☐ 203(a)(2)(A) Spouse - F2-1 ☐ 203(a)(3) Married S/D - F3-1	
Completed	☐ 201(b) Parent - IR-5 ☐ 203(a)(2)(A) Child - F2-2 ☐ 203(a)(4) Brother/Sister - F4-1	
Approved	Petition was filed on (Priority Date mm/dd/yyyy):	☐ Field Investigation ☐ Personal Interview ☐ 204(a)(2)(A) Resolved
		☐ Previously Forwarded ☐ Pet. A-File Reviewed ☐ I-485 Filed Simultaneously
Returned	PDR request granted/denied - New priority date (mm/dd/yyyy):	☐ 203(g) Resolved ☐ Ben. A-File Reviewed ☐ 204(g) Resolved
Remarks		

At which USCIS office (e.g., NBC, VSC, LOS, CRO) was Form I-130 adjudicated? ______

To be completed by an attorney or accredited representative (if any).

☒ Select this box if Form G-28 is attached.	Volag Number (if any)	Attorney State Bar Number (if applicable)	Attorney or Accredited Representative USCIS Online Account Number (if any)

▶ **START HERE - Type or print in black ink.**

If you need extra space to complete any section of this petition, use the space provided in Part 9. Additional Information. **Complete and submit as many copies of Part 9., as necessary, with your petition.**

Part 1. Relationship (You are the Petitioner. Your relative is the Beneficiary)

1. I am filing this petition for my (Select only one box):
☐ Spouse ☒ Parent ☐ Brother/Sister ☐ Child

2. If you are filing this petition for your child or parent, select the box that describes your relationship (Select only one box):
☐ Child was born to parents who were married to each other at the time of the child's birth
☐ Stepchild/Stepparent
☐ Child was born to parents who were not married to each other at the time of the child's birth
☐ Child was adopted (not an Orphan or Hague Convention adoptee)

3. If the beneficiary is your brother/sister, are you related by adoption? ☐ Yes ☒ No

4. Did you gain lawful permanent resident status or citizenship through adoption? ☐ Yes ☒ No

Part 2. Information About You (Petitioner)

1. Alien Registration Number (A-Number) (if any)
▶ A-

2. USCIS Online Account Number (if any)
▶

3. U.S. Social Security Number (if any)
▶

Your Full Name

4.a. Family Name (Last Name)

4.b. Given Name (First Name)

4.c. Middle Name

Part 2. Information About You (Petitioner) (continued)

Other Names Used (if any)

Provide all other names you have ever used, including aliases, maiden name, and nicknames.

5.a. Family Name (Last Name): None

5.b. Given Name (First Name):

5.c. Middle Name:

Other Information

6. City/Town/Village of Birth: [redacted]

7. C of Birth: Philippines

8. Date of Birth (mm/dd/yyyy): 10/01/1966

9. Sex ☒ Male ☐ Female

Mailing Address

10.a. In Care Of Name: [redacted]

10.b. S and Name: [redacted]

10.c. ☐ Apt. ☐ Ste. ☐ Flr.

10.d. City or Town: Long Beach

10.e. State: CA **10.f.** ZIP Code: 90806

10.g. Province:

10.h. Postal Code:

10.i. Country: USA

11. Is your current mailing address the same as your physical address? ☐ Yes ☒ No

If you answered "No" to **Item Number 11.**, provide information on your physical address in **Item Numbers 12.a. - 13.b.**

Address History

Provide your physical addresses for the last five years, whether inside or outside the United States. Provide your current address first if it is different from your mailing address in **Item Numbers 10.a. - 10.i.**

Physical Address 1

12.a. Street Number and Name: [redacted]

12.b. ☒ Apt. ☐ Ste. ☐ Flr. 7

12.c. City or Town: Long Beach

12.d. State: CA **12.e.** ZIP Code: 908 06

12.f. Province:

12.g. Postal Code:

12.h. Country: USA

13.a. Date From (mm/dd/yyyy): 12/28/2009

13.b. Date To (mm/dd/yyyy): PRESENT

Physical Address 2

14.a. Street Number and Name:

14.b. ☐ Apt. ☐ Ste. ☐ Flr.

14.c. City or Town:

14.d. State: **14.e.** ZIP Code:

14.f. Province:

14.g. Postal Code:

14.h. Country:

15.a. Date From (mm/dd/yyyy):

15.b. Date To (mm/dd/yyyy):

Your Marital Information

16. How many times have you been married? ► 1

17. Current Marital Status

☐ Single, Never Married ☐ Married ☒ Divorced ☐ Widowed ☐ Separated ☐ Annulled

Part 2. Information About You (Petitioner) (continued)

18. Date of Current Marriage (if currently married) (mm/dd/yyyy)

Place of Your Current Marriage (if married)

19.a. City or Town

19.b. State

19.c. Province

19.d. Country

Names of All Your Spouses (if any)

Provide information on your current spouse (if currently married) first and then list all your prior spouses (if any).

Spouse 1

20.a. Family Name (Last Name)

20.b. Given Name (First Name)

20.c. Middle Name

21. Date Marriage Ended (mm/dd/yyyy) 09/29/2014

Spouse 2

22.a. Family Name (Last Name)

22.b. Given Name (First Name)

22.c. Middle Name

23. Date Marriage Ended (mm/dd/yyyy)

Information About Your Parents

Parent 1's Information

Full Name of Parent 1

24.a. Family Name (Last Name)

24.b. Given Name (First Name)

24.c. Middle Name

25. Date of Birth (mm/dd/yyyy) 10/19/1945

26. Sex ☒ Male ☐ Female

27. Country of Birth

28. City/Town/Village of Residence

29. Country of Residence

Parent 2's Information

Full Name of Parent 2

30.a. Family Name (Last Name)

30.b. Given Name (First Name)

30.c. Middle Name

31. Date of Birth (mm/dd/yyyy) 08/05/1948

32. Sex ☐ Male ☒ Female

33. Country of Birth

Philippines

34. City/Town/Village of Residence

35. Country of Residence

Philippines

Additional Information About You (Petitioner)

36. I am a (Select **only one** box):

☒ U.S. Citizen ☐ Lawful Permanent Resident

If you are a U.S. citizen, complete Item Number 37.

37. My citizenship was acquired through (Select **only one** box):

☐ Birth in the United States

☒ Naturalization

☐ Parents

38. Have you obtained a Certificate of Naturalization or a Certificate of Citizenship? ☒ Yes ☐ No

If you answered "Yes" to **Item Number 38.**, complete the following:

39.a. Certificate Number

39.b. Place of Issuance

Los Angeles, CA

39.c. Date of Issuance (mm/dd/yyyy) 09/18/2018

Part 2. Information About You (Petitioner) (continued)

If you are a lawful permanent resident, complete Item Numbers 40.a. - 41.

40.a. Class of Admission

40.b. Date of Admission (mm/dd/yyyy)

Place of Admission

40.c. City or Town

40.d State

41. Did you gain lawful permanent resident status through marriage to a U.S. citizen or lawful permanent resident?

☐ Yes ☐ No

Employment History

Provide your employment history for the last five years, whether inside or outside the United States. Provide your current employment first. If you are currently unemployed, type or print "Unemployed" in Item Number 42.

Employer 1

42. Name of Employer/Company [redacted]

43.a. Street Number and Name [redacted]

43.b. ☐ Apt. ☐ Ste. ☐ Flr.

43.c. City or Town Long Beach

43.d. State CA 43.e. ZIP Code 90813

43.f. Province

43.g. Postal Code

43.h. Country USA

44. Your Occupation [redacted]

45.a. Date From (mm/dd/yyyy) 07/30/2007

45.b. Date To (mm/dd/yyyy) PRESENT

Employer 2

46. Name of Employer/Company

47.a. Street Number and Name

47.b. ☐ Apt. ☐ Ste. ☐ Flr.

47.c. City or Town

47.d. State 47.e. ZIP Code

47.f. Province

47.g. Postal Code

47.h. Country

48. Your Occupation

49.a. Date From (mm/dd/yyyy)

49.b. Date To (mm/dd/yyyy)

Part 3. Biographic Information

NOTE: Provide the biographic information about you, the petitioner.

1. Ethnicity (Select **only one** box)

☐ Hispanic or Latino
☒ Not Hispanic or Latino

2. Race (Select **all applicable** boxes)

☐ White
☒ Asian
☐ Black or African American
☐ American Indian or Alaska Native
☒ Native Hawaiian or Other Pacific Islander

3. Height Feet 5 Inches 7

4. Weight Pounds 1 8 5

5. Eye Color (Select **only one** box)

☐ Black ☐ Blue ☒ Brown
☐ Gray ☐ Green ☐ Hazel
☐ Maroon ☐ Pink ☐ Unknown/Other

Part 3. Biographic Information (continued)

6. Hair Color (Select only one box)

☒ Bald (No hair) ☐ Black ☐ Blond
☐ Brown ☐ Gray ☐ Red
☐ Sandy ☐ White ☐ Unknown/Other

Part 4. Information About Beneficiary

1. Alien Registration Number (A-Number) (if any)
▶ A-

2. USCIS Online Account Number (if any)
▶

3. U.S. Social Security Number (if any)
▶

Beneficiary's Full Name

4.a. Family Name (Last Name)

4.b. Given Name (First Name)

4.c. Middle Name

Other Names Used (if any)

Provide all other names the beneficiary has ever used, including aliases, maiden name, and nicknames.

5.a. Family Name (Last Name) None

5.b. Given Name (First Name)

5.c. Middle Name

Other Information About Beneficiary

6. City/Town/Village of Birth

7. Country of Birth
Philippines

8. Date of Birth (mm/dd/yyyy) 08/05/1948

9. Sex ☐ Male ☒ Female

10. Has anyone else ever filed a petition for the beneficiary?
☐ Yes ☒ No ☐ Unknown

NOTE: Select "Unknown" *only* if you do not know, and the beneficiary also does not know, if anyone else has ever filed a petition for the beneficiary.

Beneficiary's Physical Address

If the beneficiary lives outside the United States in a home without a street number or name, leave **Item Numbers 11.a.** and **11.b.** blank.

11.a. Street Number and Name

11.b. ☐ Apt. ☐ Ste. ☐ Flr.

11.c. City or Town

11.d. State 11.e. ZIP Code

11.f. Province

11.g. Postal Code

11.h. Country
Philippines

Other Address and Contact Information

Provide the address in the United States where the beneficiary intends to live, if different from **Item Numbers 11.a. - 11.h.** If the address is the same, type or print "SAME" in **Item Number 12.a.**

12.a Street Number and Name

12.b. ☒ Apt. ☐ Ste. ☐ Flr. 7

12.c. City or Town Long Beach

12.d. State CA 12.e. ZIP Code

Provide the beneficiary's address outside the United States, if different from **Item Numbers 11.a. - 11.h.** If the address is the same, type or print "SAME" in **Item Number 13.a.**

13.a. Street Number and Name SAME

13.b. ☐ Apt. ☐ Ste. ☐ Flr.

13.c. City or Town

13.d. Province

13.e. Postal Code

13.f. Country

14. Daytime Telephone Number (if any)

Part 4. Information About Beneficiary (continued)

15. [redacted] Number (if any)

16. Email Address (if any)

Beneficiary's Marital Information

17. How many times has the beneficiary been married? ▶ 1

18. Current Marital Status

☐ Single, Never Married ☒ Married ☐ Divorced ☐ Widowed ☐ Separated ☐ Annulled

19. Date of Current Marriage (if currently married) (mm/dd/yyyy) 10/05/1965

Place of Beneficiary's Current Marriage (if married)

20.a. City or Town

20.b. State

20.c. Province

20.d. Country Philippines

Names of Beneficiary's Spouses (if any)

Provide information on the beneficiary's current spouse (if currently married) first and then list all the beneficiary's prior spouses (if any).

Spouse 1

21.a. Family Name (Last Name) None

21.b. Given Name (First Name)

21.c. Middle Name

22. Date Marriage Ended (mm/dd/yyyy)

Spouse 2

23.a. Family Name (Last Name)

23.b. Given Name (First Name)

23.c. Middle Name

24. Date Marriage Ended (mm/dd/yyyy)

Information About Beneficiary's Family

Provide information about the beneficiary's spouse and children.

Person 1

25.a. Family Name (Last Name)

25.b. Given Name (First Name)

25.c. Middle Name

26. Relationship Child

27. Date of Birth (mm/dd/yyyy) 10/01/1966

28. Country of Birth Philippines

Person 2

29.a. Family Name (Last Name)

29.b. Given Name (First Name)

29.c. Middle Name

30. Relationship Child

31. Date of Birth (mm/dd/yyyy) 12/25/1967

32. Country of Birth Philippines

Person 3

33.a. Family Name (Last Name)

33.b. Given Name (First Name)

33.c. Middle Name

34. Relationship Child

35. Date of Birth (mm/dd/yyyy) 09/18/1969

36. Country of Birth Philippines

Part 4. Information About Beneficiary (continued)

Person 4

37.a. Family Name (Last Name)

37.b. Given Name (First Name)

37.c. Middle Name

38. Relationship

39. Date of Birth (mm/dd/yyyy)

40. Country of Birth

Person 5

41.a. Family Name (Last Name)

41.b. Given Name (First Name)

41.c. Middle Name

42. Relationship

43. Date of Birth (mm/dd/yyyy)

44. Country of Birth

Beneficiary's Entry Information

45. Was the beneficiary **EVER** in the United States?

☒ Yes ☐ No

If the beneficiary is currently in the United States, complete **Items Numbers 46.a. - 46.d.**

46.a. He or she arrived as a (Class of Admission):

46.b. Form I-94 Arrival-Departure Record Number

▶

46.c. Date of Arrival (mm/dd/yyyy)

46.d. Date authorized stay expired, or will expire, as shown on Form I-94 or Form I-95 (mm/dd/yyyy) or type or print "D/S" for Duration of Status

47. Passport Number

P0107860A

48. Travel Document Number

49. Country of Issuance for Passport or Travel Document

Philippines

50. Expiration Date for Passport or Travel Document (mm/dd/yyyy)

10/03/2021

Beneficiary's Employment Information

Provide the beneficiary's current employment information (if applicable), even if they are employed outside of the United States. If the beneficiary is currently unemployed, type or print "Unemployed" in **Item Number 51.a.**

51.a. Name of Current Employer (if applicable)

Unemployed

51.b. Street Number and Name

51.c. ☐ Apt. ☐ Ste. ☐ Flr.

51.d. City or Town

51.e. State **51.f.** ZIP Code

51.g. Province

51.h. Postal Code

51.i. Country

52. Date Employment Began (mm/dd/yyyy)

Additional Information About Beneficiary

53. Was the beneficiary **EVER** in immigration proceedings?

☐ Yes ☒ No

54. If you answered "Yes," select the type of proceedings and provide the location and date of the proceedings.

☐ Removal ☐ Exclusion/Deportation

☐ Rescission ☐ Other Judicial Proceedings

55.a. City or Town

55.b. State

56. Date (mm/dd/yyyy)

Part 4. Information About Beneficiary (continued)

If the beneficiary's native written language does not use Roman letters, type or print his or her name and foreign address in their native written language.

57.a. Family Name (Last Name)

57.b. Given Name (First Name)

57.c. Middle Name

58.a. Street Number and Name

58.b. ☐ Apt. ☐ Ste. ☐ Flr.

58.c. City or Town

58.d. Province

58.e. Postal Code

58.f. Country

If filing for your spouse, provide the last address at which you physically lived together. If you never lived together, type or print, "Never lived together" in Item Number 59.a.

59.a. Street Number and Name

59.b. ☐ Apt. ☐ Ste. ☐ Flr.

59.c. City or Town

59.d. State **59.e.** ZIP Code

59.f. Province

59.g. Postal Code

59.h. Country

60.a. Date From (mm/dd/yyyy)

60.b. Date To (mm/dd/yyyy)

The beneficiary is in the United States and will apply for adjustment of status to that of a lawful permanent resident at the U.S. Citizenship and Immigration Services (USCIS) office in:

61.a. City or Town

61.b. State

The beneficiary will not apply for adjustment of status in the United States, but he or she will apply for an immigrant visa abroad at the U.S. Embassy or U.S. Consulate in:

62.a. City or Town

62.b. Province

62.c. Country

Philippines

NOTE: Choosing a U.S. Embassy or U.S. Consulate outside the country of the beneficiary's last residence does not guarantee that it will accept the beneficiary's case for processing. In these situations, the designated U.S. Embassy or U.S. Consulate has discretion over whether or not to accept the beneficiary's case.

Part 5. Other Information

1. Have you EVER previously filed a petition for this beneficiary or any other alien? ☐ Yes ☒ No

If you answered "Yes," provide the name, place, date of filing, and the result.

2.a. Family Name (Last Name)

2.b. Given Name (First Name)

2.c. Middle Name

3.a. City or Town

3.b. State

4. Date Filed (mm/dd/yyyy)

5. Result (for example, approved, denied, withdrawn)

If you are also submitting separate petitions for other relatives, provide the names of and your relationship to each relative.

Relative 1

6.a. Family Name (Last Name)

6.b. Given Name (First Name)

6.c. Middle Name

7. Relationship

Part 5. Other Information (continued)

Relative 2

8.a. Family Name (Last Name)

8.b. Given Name (First Name)

8.c. Middle Name

9. Relationship

WARNING: USCIS investigates the claimed relationships and verifies the validity of documents you submit. If you falsify a family relationship to obtain a visa, USCIS may seek to have you criminally prosecuted.

PENALTIES: By law, you may be imprisoned for up to 5 years or fined $250,000, or both, for entering into a marriage contract in order to evade any U.S. immigration law. In addition, you may be fined up to $10,000 and imprisoned for up to 5 years, or both, for knowingly and willfully falsifying or concealing a material fact or using any false document in submitting this petition.

Part 6. Petitioner's Statement, Contact Information, Declaration, and Signature

NOTE: Read the Penalties section of the Form I-130 Instructions before completing this part.

Petitioner's Statement

NOTE: Select the box for either **Item Number 1.a.** or **1.b.** If applicable, select the box for **Item Number 2.**

1.a. [X] I can read and understand English, and I have read and understand every question and instruction on this petition and my answer to every question.

1.b. [ ] The interpreter named in **Part 7.** read to me every question and instruction on this petition and my answer to every question in ______, a language in which I am fluent. I understood all of this information as interpreted.

2. [X] At my request, the preparer named in **Part 8.**, ______, prepared this petition for me based only upon information I provided or authorized.

Petitioner's Contact Information

3. Petitioner's Daytime Telephone Number

4. Petitioner's Mobile Telephone Number (if any)

5. Petitioner's Email Address (if any)

Petitioner's Declaration and Certification

Copies of any documents I have submitted are exact photocopies of unaltered, original documents, and I understand that USCIS may require that I submit original documents to USCIS at a later date. Furthermore, I authorize the release of any information from any of my records that USCIS may need to determine my eligibility for the immigration benefit I seek.

I further authorize release of information contained in this petition, in supporting documents, and in my USCIS records to other entities and persons where necessary for the administration and enforcement of U.S. immigration laws.

I understand that USCIS may require me to appear for an appointment to take my biometrics (fingerprints, photograph, and/or signature) and, at that time, if I am required to provide biometrics, I will be required to sign an oath reaffirming that:

1) I provided or authorized all of the information contained in, and submitted with, my petition;

2) I reviewed and understood all of the information in, and submitted with, my petition; and

3) All of this information was complete, true, and correct at the time of filing.

I certify, under penalty of perjury, that all of the information in my petition and any document submitted with it were provided or authorized by me, that I reviewed and understand all of the information contained in, and submitted with, my petition, and that all of this information is complete, true, and correct.

Petitioner's Signature

6.a. Petitioner's Signature (sign in ink)

6.b. Date of Signature (mm/dd/yyyy) 11 1 18

NOTE TO ALL PETITIONERS: If you do not completely fill out this petition or fail to submit required documents listed in the Instructions, USCIS may deny your petition.

Part 7. Interpreter's Contact Information, Certification, and Signature

Provide the following information about the interpreter if you used one.

Interpreter's Full Name

1.a. Interpreter's Family Name (Last Name)

1.b. Interpreter's Given Name (First Name)

2. Interpreter's Business or Organization Name (if any)

Interpreter's Mailing Address

3.a. Street Number and Name

3.b. ☐ Apt. ☐ Ste. ☐ Flr.

3.c. City or Town

3.d. State 3.e. ZIP Code

3.f. Province

3.g. Postal Code

3.h. Country

Interpreter's Contact Information

4. Interpreter's Daytime Telephone Number

5. Interpreter's Mobile Telephone Number (if any)

6. Interpreter's Email Address (if any)

Interpreter's Certification

I certify, under penalty of perjury, that:

I am fluent in English and ______,

which is the same language provided in **Part 6., Item Number 1.b.**, and I have read to this petitioner in the identified language every question and instruction on this petition and his or her answer to every question. The petitioner informed me that he or she understands every instruction, question, and answer on the petition, including the **Petitioner's Declaration and Certification**, and has verified the accuracy of every answer.

Interpreter's Signature

7.a. Interpreter's Signature (sign in ink)

7.b. Date of Signature (mm/dd/yyyy)

Part 8. Contact Information, Declaration, and Signature of the Person Preparing this Petition, if Other Than the Petitioner

Provide the following information about the preparer.

Preparer's Full Name

1.a. Preparer's Family Name (Last Name)

1.b. Preparer's Given Name (First Name)

2. Preparer's Business or Organization Name (if any)
Law Offices of Brian D. Lerner, APC

Preparer's Mailing Address

3.a. Street Number and Name 3233 E. Broadway

3.b. ☐ Apt. ☐ Ste. ☐ Flr.

3.c. City or Town Long Beach

3.d. State CA 3.e. ZIP Code 90803

3.f. Province

3.g. Postal Code

3.h. Country
USA

Part 8. Contact Information, Declaration, and Signature of the Person Preparing this Petition, if Other Than the Petitioner (continued)

Preparer's Contact Information

4. Preparer's Daytime Telephone Number

(562) 495-0554

5. Preparer's Mobile Telephone Number (if any)

6. Preparer's Email Address (if any)

Preparer's Statement

7.a. ☐ I am not an attorney or accredited representative but have prepared this petition on behalf of the petitioner and with the petitioner's consent.

7.b. ☒ I am an attorney or accredited representative and my representation of the petitioner in this case ☒ extends ☐ does not extend beyond the preparation of this petition.

NOTE: If you are an attorney or accredited representative whose representation extends beyond preparation of this petition, you may be obliged to submit a completed Form G-28, Notice of Entry of Appearance as Attorney or Accredited Representative, with this petition.

Preparer's Certification

By my signature, I certify, under penalty of perjury, that I prepared this petition at the request of the petitioner. The petitioner then reviewed this completed petition and informed me that he or she understands all of the information contained in, and submitted with, his or her petition, including the **Petitioner's Declaration and Certification**, and that all of this information is complete, true, and correct. I completed this petition based only on information that the petitioner provided to me or authorized me to obtain or use.

Preparer's Signature

8.a.

8.b. Date of Signature (mm/dd/yyyy) 11/2/12

Part 9. Additional Information

If you need extra space to provide any additional information within this petition, use the space below. If you need more space than what is provided, you may make copies of this page to complete and file with this petition or attach a separate sheet of paper. Type or print your name and A-Number (if any) at the top of each sheet; indicate the **Page Number, Part Number,** and **Item Number** to which your answer refers; and sign and date each sheet.

1.a. Family Name (Last Name) [redacted]

1.b. Given Name (First Name) [redacted]

1.c. Middle Name [redacted]

2. A-Number (if any) ► A- [redacted]

3.a. Page Number **3.b.** Part Number **3.c.** Item Number

3.d.

4.a. Page Number **4.b.** Part Number **4.c.** Item Number

4.d.

5.a. Page Number **5.b.** Part Number **5.c.** Item Number

5.d.

6.a. Page Number **6.b.** Part Number **6.c.** Item Number

6.d.

7.a. Page Number **7.b.** Part Number **7.c.** Item Number

7.d.

EXHIBITS

EXHIBIT '1':

Petitioner's Birth Certificate

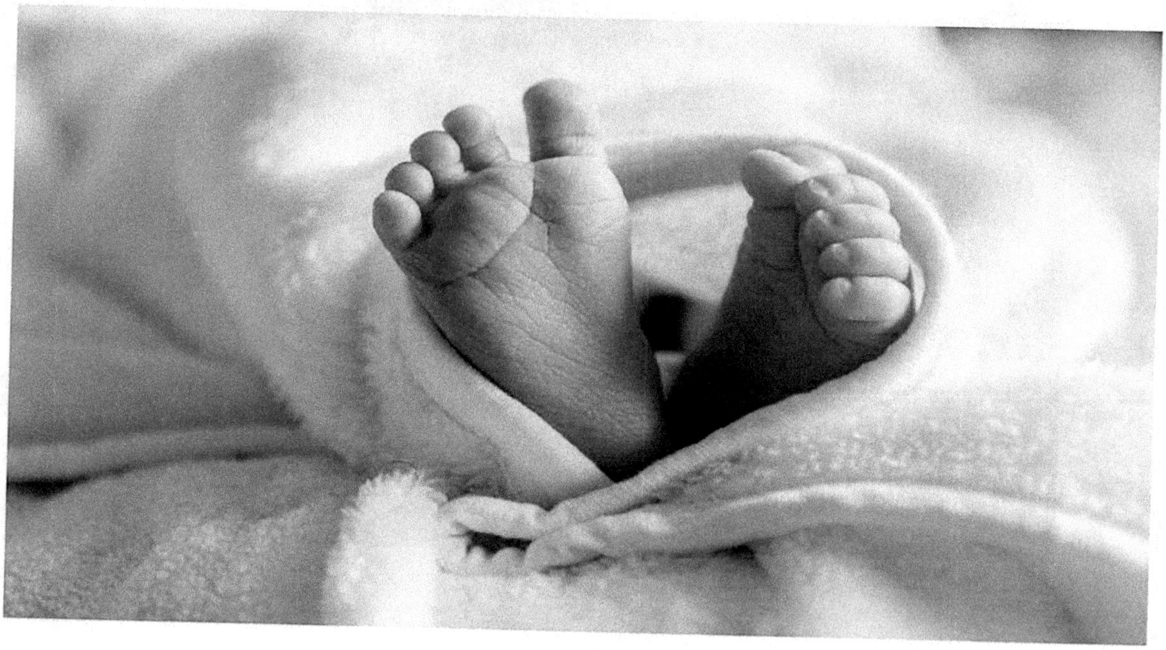

(TO BE ACCOMPLISHED IN DUPLICATE)

REPUBLIC OF THE PHILIPPINES

CERTIFICATE OF LIVE BIRTH

(FILL OUT COMPLETELY, ACCURATELY, LEGIBLY IN INK OR TYPEWRITER)

Register Number:

Province: Philippines — (a) Civil Registrar-General No.

City or Municipality: — (b) Local Civil Registrar No. 4139 (1966)

RESERVE FOR BINDING

CHILD

FATHER

MOTHER

ATTENDANT AT BIRTH

DEC 21 1966

(SPACE FOR MEDICAL AND HEALTH ITEMS FOR SPECIAL PURPOSES)

EXHIBIT '2':

Petitioner's Certificate of Naturalization

THE UNITED STATES OF AMERICA

No. 40494867

CERTIFICATE OF NATURALIZATION

USCIS Registration No. A099 639 884

Personal description of holder as of date of naturalization:

Date of birth: OCTOBER 01, 1966

Sex: MALE

Height: 5 feet 07 inches

Marital status: DIVORCED

Country of former nationality: PHILIPPINES

I certify that the description given is true, and that the photograph affixed hereto is a likeness of me.

(Complete and true signature of holder)

Be it known that, pursuant to an application filed with the Secretary of Homeland Security

at: LOS ANGELES, CALIFORNIA

The Secretary having found that:

residing at:

LONG BEACH, CALIFORNIA

having complied in all respects with all of the applicable provisions of the naturalization laws of the United States, being entitled to be admitted as a citizen of the United States, and having taken the oath of allegiance at a ceremony conducted by

US DISTRICT COURT CENTRAL DISTRICT

at: LOS ANGELES, CALIFORNIA on: SEPTEMBER 18, 2018

such person is admitted as a citizen of the United States of America.

U. S. Citizenship and Immigration Services

EXHIBIT '3':

Beneficiary's Birth Certificate

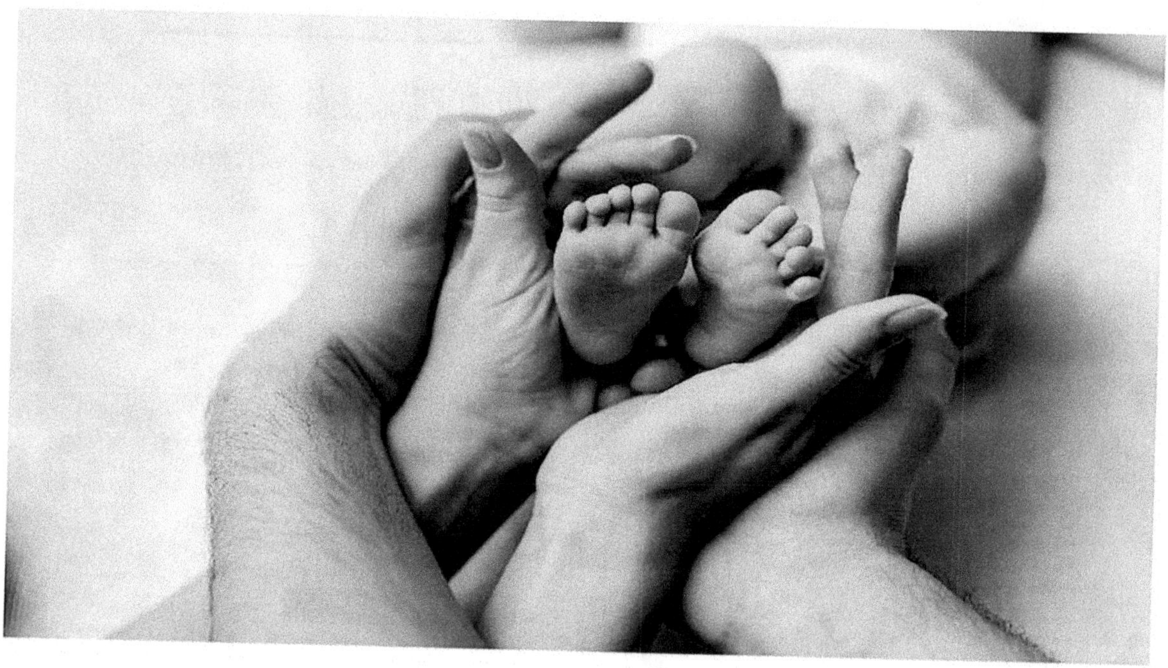

REPUBLIC OF THE PHILIPPINES
REPUBLICA DE FILIPINAS

CERTIFICATE OF BIRTH
CERTIFICADO DE NACIMIENTO

PLACE OF BIRTH
LUGAR DE NACIMIENTO

Registry No. 2985 (h48)

Sept. 1948

Municipality of Tondo

Isla de Balut

Province of 860

Beltran

Date of birth: Aug. 5 1948

Sex: Female

Nationality: Filipino

Legitimate: Yes

Father: Filipino, Age at last birthday 38 yrs

Mother: Filipino, Age at last birthday 35 yrs, Tondo, Manila, married, R. Catholic, housewife

Number of children born to this mother, including present birth: 7

Number of children of this mother now living: 6

CERTIFICATE OF ATTENDING PHYSICIAN OR MIDWIFE OR OF THE FATHER OR MOTHER*

CERTIFICADO DEL MEDICO QUE ASISTIÓ Ó DE LA COMADRONA Ó DEL PADRE Ó LA MADRE

I HEREBY CERTIFY that I
POR LA PRESENTE CERTIFICO

Registration Officer

SEP 21 1948

Local Civil Registrar—Registrador Civil Local

CITY CIVIL REGISTRAR
CITY OF MANILA

EXHIBIT '4':

Beneficiary's Foreign Passport

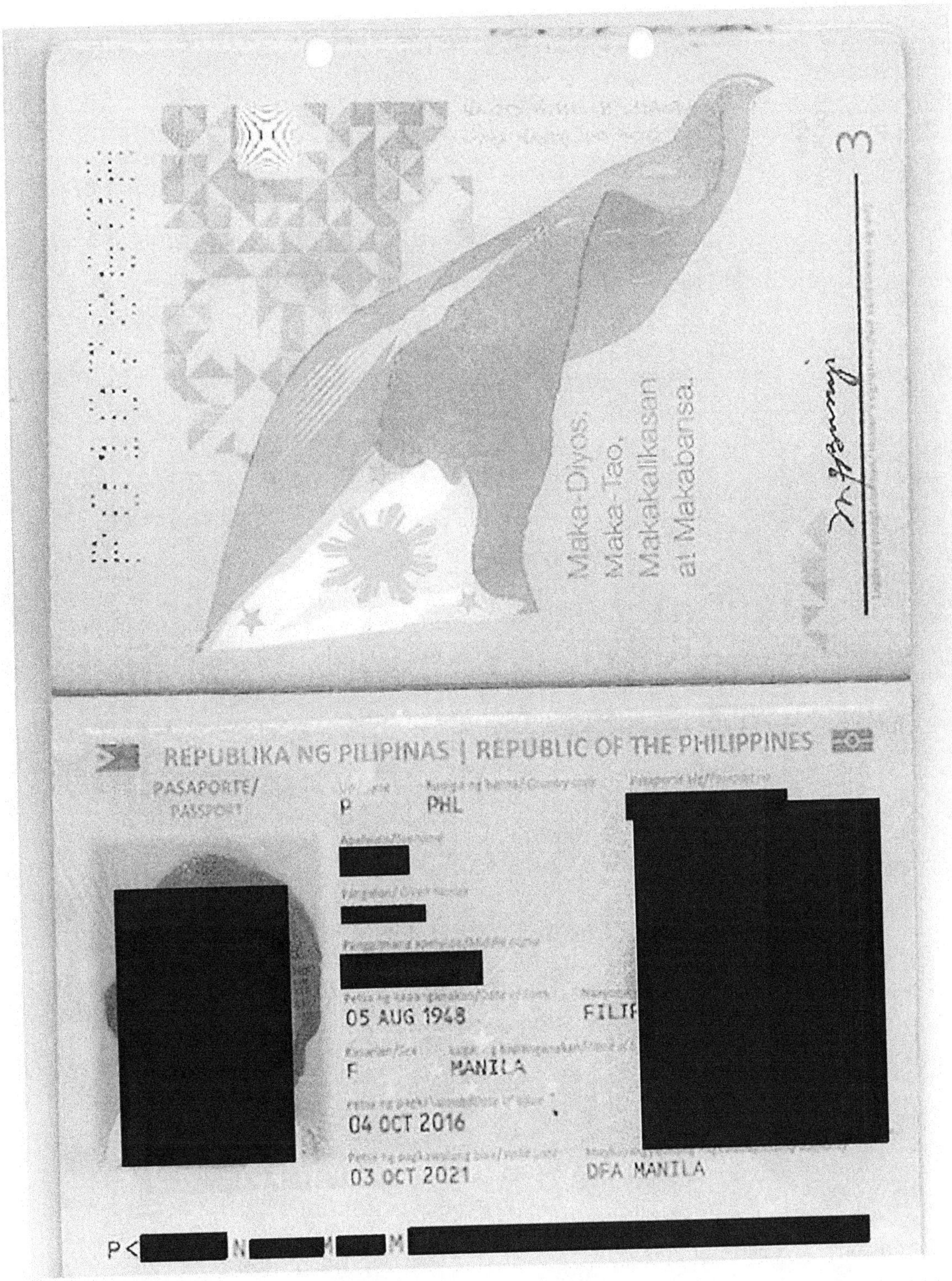
Maka-Diyos,
Maka-Tao,
Makakalikasan
at Makabansa.
3
REPUBLIKA NG PILIPINAS | REPUBLIC OF THE PHILIPPINES
PASAPORTE/
PASSPORT
P
PHL
05 AUG 1948
F
MANILA
04 OCT 2016
03 OCT 2021
DFA MANILA

EXHIBIT '5':

Beneficiary's Visa and I-94

24
ADMITTED
NOV 1 4 2017
B2
MAY 1 3 2018
ADMITTED
LAX
JUN 0 3 2018
B-2
DEC 0 2 2018
VISA
UNITED STATES
OF AMERICA
Issuing Post Name
Control Number
Surname
Given Name
Visa Type /Class
R B1/B2
Passport Number
Sex
F
Birth Date
05AUG1948
Nationality
PHIL
Entries
M
Issue Date
10OCT2017
Expiration Date
03OCT2027
Annotation
M7731641

For: [redacted]

U.S. Customs and Border Protection
Securing America's Borders

Most Recent I-94

Admission (I-94) Record Number : [redacted]
Most Recent Date of Entry: 2018 June 03
Class of Admission : B2
Admit Until Date : 12/02/2018
Details provided on the I-94 Information form:

Last/Surname :	[redacted]
First (Given) Name :	[redacted]
Birth Date :	1948 August 05
Passport Number :	[redacted]
Country of Issuance :	Philippines

Get Travel History

- Effective April 26, 2013, DHS began automating the admission process. An alien lawfully admitted or paroled into the U.S. is no longer required to be in possession of a preprinted Form I-94. A record of admission printed from the CBP website constitutes a lawful record of admission. See 8 CFR § 1.4(d).
- If an employer, local, state or federal agency requests admission information, present your admission (I-94) number along with any additional required documents requested by that employer or agency.
- Note: For security reasons, we recommend that you close your browser after you have finished retrieving your I-94 number.

For inquiries or questions regarding your I-94, please click here

Accessibility | Privacy Policy

ABOUT THE AUTHOR

Brian D. Lerner is an Immigration Lawyer and runs a National Immigration Law Firm for nearly 30 years. He is an attorney who is a certified specialist that might help in Immigration & Nationality Law as issued by the California State Bar, Board of Legal Specialization. Attorney Lerner is an expert in Immigration Law, Removal and Deportation, Citizenship, Waiver and Appeals.

He has been a licensed attorney since 1992 and started the Law Offices of Brian D. Lerner, APC. The immigration practice consists of Immigration and Nationality Law, and everything involved with and regarding immigration which includes citizenship, investment visas, family and employment visas, removal and deportation hearings, appeals, waivers, adjustment, consulate processing and all types of immigration and citizenship matters.

He has represented clients from all over the U.S. and in many countries around the world. One side of his practice is dedicated to keeping people in the U.S. and fighting for their immigration rights, while another side is to get people back who have been deported and removed from the U.S.

Also, there is the affirmative part of Immigration Law which Brian Lerner has helped numerous people come into the U.S. on business visas, investment visas, student visas, fiancée and marriage visas, religious visas and many more. Attorney Lerner has helped immigrants who are victims of crime and domestic violence or ones that are married to abusers.

In other words, Attorney Lerner has a firm that helps people all over the U.S. He has dedicated significant time to preparing numerous petitions and applications for you to get at a fraction of the price of hiring an attorney. He says it is the next best thing to a real attorney because they are real petitions prepared by an expert.

www.ingramcontent.com/pod-product-compliance
Lightning Source LLC
Chambersburg PA
CBHW061357240926
51846CB00007B/1433
9781958990193